28

	DATE DUE		

WIDE WORLD

PEOPLE *of the* MOUNTAINS

Jen Green

**RAINTREE
STECK-VAUGHN**
PUBLISHERS
The Steck-Vaughn Company

Austin, Texas

WIDE WORLD

People *of the* **DESERTS**

People *of the* **GRASSLANDS**

People *of the* **ISLANDS**

People *of the* **MOUNTAINS**

People *of the* **POLAR REGIONS**

People *of the* **RAIN FORESTS**

Cover: A young Sherpa girl holding her baby brother in the Nepalese Himalayas

Title page: A boy with a heavily laden donkey in Ladakh, northern India

This spread: Peaks of the Canadian Rocky Mountains, near Alberta

Published by Raintree Steck-Vaughn Publishers, an imprint of Steck-Vaughn Company

Library of Congress Cataloging-in-Publication Data
Green, Jen.
People of the mountains / Jen Green.
    p.   cm.—(Wide world)
    Includes bibliographical references and index.
    Summary: Examines the many different types of cultures that exist in mountainous regions, discussing settlements, houses, employment, transportation, communication, daily life, leisure activities, and tourism.
    ISBN 0-8172-5062-X
    1. Mountain people—Juvenile literature.
    2. Mountain life—Juvenile literature.
    3. Mountain ecology—Juvenile literature.
    [1. Mountain life.]
    I. Title. II. Series.
    GN392.G74   1998
    306'.09143—dc21   97-33223

Printed in Italy. Bound in the United States.
1 2 3 4 5 6 7 8 9 0 02 01 00 99 98

The author would like to dedicate this book to Liz, with many memories of mountains.

Contents

Introduction

The highest mountains

Asia: Everest, 29,029 ft. (8,848 m)
South America: Aconcagua, 22,835 ft. (6,960 m)
North America: McKinley, 20,322 ft. (6,194 m)
Africa: Kilimanjaro, 19,341 ft. (5,895 m)
Europe: Elbrus, 18,481 ft. (5,633 m)
Australia: Mount Cook, 12,349 ft. (3,764 m)
Antarctica: Vinson Massif, 16,860 ft. (5,139 m)

▼ A young boy in Ladakh, northern India

The craggy beauty of snow-capped mountains inspires a sense of awe in many people. "A hundred ages would not be enough to describe all the wonders of the Himalayas," an Indian proverb claims. In the past, many peoples thought of the mountains as divine. The ancient Greeks believed that their gods lived on Mount Olympus. In Japan, Tibet, and Indonesia, people prayed to the gods from the high peaks.

As well as believing that mountains were special and sacred, people found the scenery forbidding, even terrifying. Nowadays we no longer fear the mountains in the same way. Great cities, especially in South America and the United States, have grown up in mountain regions. Tourists visit for sports and exercise or for sightseeing. With new roads and modern transportation such as cars and airplanes, areas that were once remote are now relatively easy to visit.

Mountain Legends

In the past, many people believed that demons or monsters haunted the mountains. In 1760, villagers told a Swiss scientist that dragons lived near the top of Mont Blanc, in the French Alps. The yeti, a mysterious creature that is half-ape and half-human, is said to live in the Himalayas. In China, there are stories of laughing mountain creatures covered with red hair.

Mountain peoples

Until recently, many mountain peoples were very isolated. In winter they were cut off from the lowlands by heavy snow. Mountain people became hardy and independent and developed their own customs. Today in some mountain regions, especially in Asia and South America, people still have hard lives. Most people in the Himalayas and high Andes are poor farmers, struggling to grow food on the steep, stony slopes. In other parts of the world, such as Europe, the United States, and Canada, people in mountain regions have lifestyles similar to people in lowland areas.

▼ Basques, who live in the Spanish Pyrenees, have preserved their traditional way of life. The Basques would like to have their own country.

The World's High Places

Map labels: Norwegian, Rockies, Appalachian, Andes, Pyrenees, Alps, Atlas, Ethiopian Plateau, Great Rift Valley, Drakensburg, Caucasus, Urals, Altai, Hindu Kush, Tibetan Plateau, HIMALAYAS, Great Dividing Range, Southern Alps

▲ This map shows the world's major mountain ranges. The Appalachians, in North America, were formed 400 million years ago. Younger ranges, such as the Andes, were formed about 10 million years ago.

A mountain is a high, steep-sided area of land that stands out above the surrounding lowlands. Mountains are found on every continent of the world. The highest are grouped in long chains, called mountain ranges.

Mountains are formed from movements of the huge plates of rock that make up the earth's crust. These plates float on the hotter, more liquid rock below. One plate may carry both the continent and the ocean bed. Over millions of years, these plates move slowly together and eventually collide with one another. Where plates collide, rock crumples up to form mountains. Elsewhere, liquid rock from inside the earth forces its way up between the plates to form volcanoes.

How mountains are formed

Fold mountain

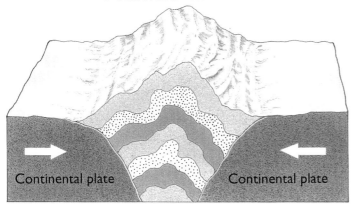

▲ When two plates under continents collide, rocks are squeezed up into fold mountains.

Volcanic mountain

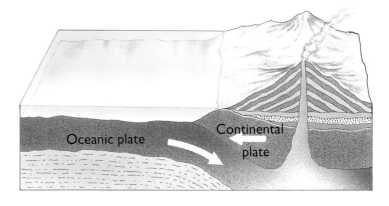

▲ When an oceanic plate is forced under a continental plate, it melts. The molten rock rises to the surface to form a volcano.

Mountain landscapes

Mountains are constantly being eroded by natural forces such as frost, rain, ice, and wind. Ice forms glaciers in high mountain valleys. As the glaciers move slowly downward, they scrape away the rocks beneath, making larger valleys. Millions of years ago, when the world's climate was much colder, glaciers were vast and very powerful.

▼ A group of walkers on the Bossons glacier, near Chamonix, in the French Alps

Climate and weather

Mountains have cold climates. Air higher up holds less oxygen and less heat. Every 500 ft. (150 m), the temperature drops 1.8° F (1° C). This is why the tops of high mountains, even ones near the equator such as Mount Kilimanjaro in Africa, are covered with ice and snow all year round.

In mountain regions, summers are short and winters are long and harsh. During the day, it may feel warm in the bright sunlight, but when the sun sets, temperatures drop to well below freezing. The daily weather can change very quickly and can be difficult to predict. Travelers setting out in clear weather may find clouds gathering quickly, bringing rain or snow. Mists can descend on mountain peaks in minutes, completely blotting out the view.

Rainfall

Rain falls on different parts of a mountain according to the direction of the main winds. Warm winds blowing from the sea contain moisture. As air is forced up the mountainside, the moisture condenses to form rain, hail, or snow. The opposite slope is often dry and barren. This is known as the rain shadow.

▼ This diagram shows the rain shadow effect, where rain falls according to the direction of the main winds.

Clouds form and rain falls.

Winds have less moisture, so little rain falls.

Winds rise over mountains and are cooled.

Warm, moist ocean winds

Rain Shadow

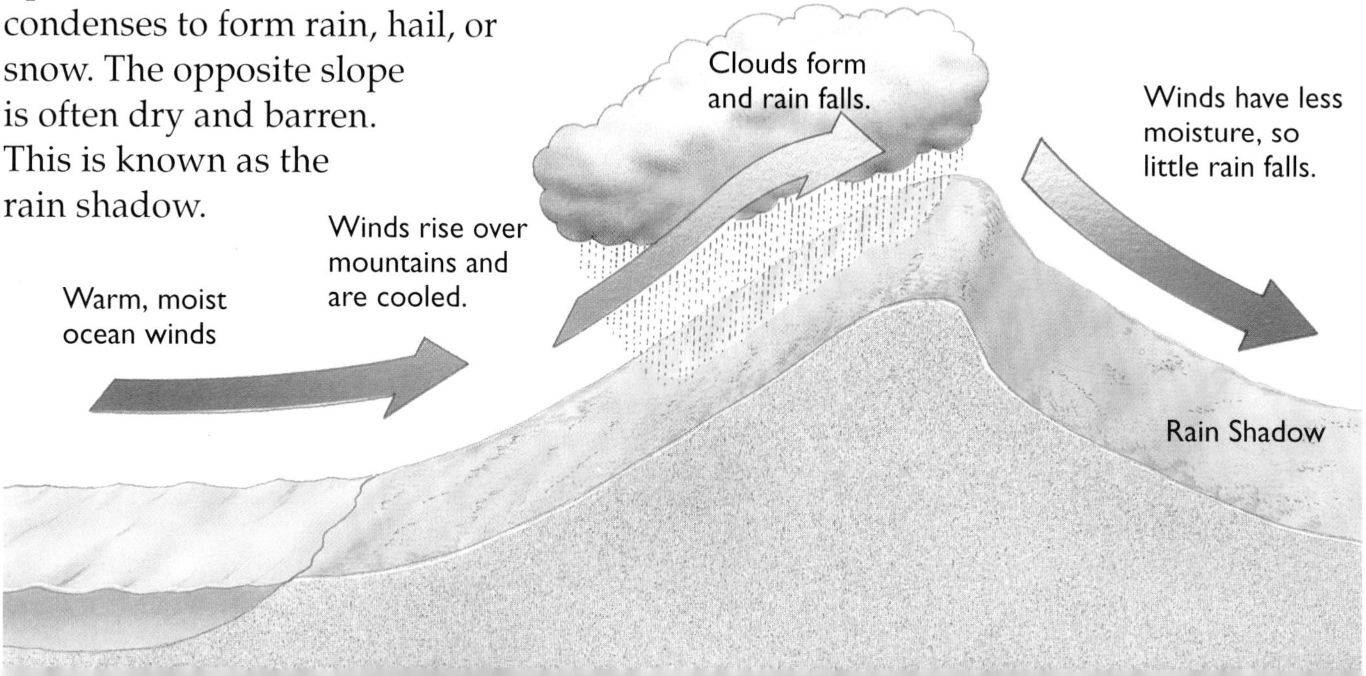

Thin Air
The lack of oxygen high up in the mountains means that visitors from lowland areas may suffer from "mountain sickness." They feel sick, dizzy, and out of breath. Local mountain people, such as the Sherpas of Nepal or the Quechua Indians of the Andes (below), are used to the high altitude so they do not get mountain sickness.

History of Mountain People

Despite the harsh conditions, people have lived in many of the world's high mountains for thousands of years. Tools and weapons found in the Alps show that Neanderthals lived there 50,000 years ago. These early hunters died out 30,000 years ago, but after the last ice age ended, modern humans settled in the same region.

During the Copper Age (4000–2200 B.C.), settlers in the Alps grew wheat and barley and herded sheep and cattle. They built villages at the foot of mountain passes and by high lakes, such as Lake Geneva in Switzerland and Lake Garda in Italy. They made copper tools and carved sacred stones in village workshops. Neolithic knives and scrapers left by mountain hunters have been discovered 13,000 ft. (4,000 m) up in the remote Chang Tang area of the Tibetan plateau.

Secrets of the "Iceman"
In 1991, a couple hiking by a glacier in the Austrian Alps stumbled upon the mummified remains of a 5,000-year-old human body. Nearby lay a copper ax, a long bow, and a deerskin case with arrows. Archaeologists believe this Copper-Age traveler may have been a shepherd, overcome by exhaustion or bad weather while climbing the high mountain pass.

◀ The body of the "Iceman" had been so well preserved by the glacier that remains of his clothing, including a woven grass cape and shoes, were also found.

The empire of the Incas

There is little evidence of the art and culture of ancient mountain people. The Incas, who lived in the Andes between A.D. 1100 and 1530, are an exception. The Inca empire was centered on the city of Cuzco, in modern Peru. The Incas built a paved road 3,231 mi. (5,200 km) long to link distant parts of their kingdom. They cut terraces in the steep Andean mountainsides to make tiny fields to farm. In the 1530s, the Incas were conquered by Spanish *conquistadors*, who took their gold and forced them into slavery. Many were sent to work in Spanish silver mines in Bolivia.

▲ The remains of the ancient city of Machu Picchu, 7,875 ft. (2,400 m) up in the Andes. The city became a refuge for the Inca people during the Spanish conquest. It was only discovered in 1911, by the American archaeologist Hiram Bingham.

Trading routes

In early medieval times, a network of unpaved roads criss-crossed Europe. Merchants traveled these rough paths with caravans of pack animals, bringing much-needed goods to villages and towns. Many of these trading routes had high passes that led through the mountains. These passes were open in summer, but were closed by snow in winter. Where the passes were narrowest, local landowners often built castles to defend their territory.

Different Languages

French, German, Italian, and a dialect, Romansh, are all spoken today in the mountains of Switzerland. In many areas, villagers speak a different language from their neighbors in the next valley. Some valleys even have their own local dialects.

Isolated villages

By the late Middle Ages, most of the great towns and cities of Europe had grown up in lowland areas, where the climate was milder, the soil was more fertile, and where there was space to build. Settlements in mountain areas stayed small—communities of farmers scratching out a living from the thin soil. Villages were isolated and became self-reliant. They developed their own customs, traditions, and even their own languages.

▼ A fortress town in Morocco. Many fortress towns were built in the Atlas Mountains of North Africa to control the trading routes across the Sahara.

▲ A painting of the St. Gotthard Pass in 1804, by the famous painter J.M.W. Turner

New roads and railroads

In the nineteenth century, new roads and railroads began to open up the mountains of Europe and North America. In the 1880s, the donkey path that crossed the Alps by the St. Gotthard Pass, at the height of 6,876 ft. (2,096 m), was replaced by a paved road. The new road made travel easier between Switzerland and Italy.

▲ A pioneer wagon train crossing Idaho about 1885. The easiest route across the Rocky Mountains was the Overland Trail, which climbed to 7,365 ft. (2,245 m).

In the late nineteenth century pioneers in covered wagons made their way across the Rocky Mountains to settle the western states of the United States. Uncharted routes, flooding, snow, and landslides made conditions very difficult, and many pioneers lost their lives on their way west. In the 1860s, the Union Pacific Railroad was the first to cross the Rocky Mountains, helping to join the east and west coasts of the United States.

Mountain life in Europe and North America changed quickly after the new roads and railroads were built. In contrast, the first Europeans to visit remote mountain regions such as the Himalayas found people whose lifestyles had changed little for hundreds of years.

Near Mount Everest in the ▶ high Himalayas, Sherpas still use caravans of yaks to transport heavy loads. The area was unknown to Europeans until about 100 years ago.

Mountain wars

Mountains form natural barriers, and many mountain ranges—such as the Pyrenees between France and Spain—mark the borders of neighboring countries. Both in the past and in recent times, mountain regions have often become disputed land, claimed by several countries as their own. Today the territory of Kashmir in central Asia is claimed by both India and Pakistan. Mountains have also been the scene of fighting because, in times of war, soldiers often retreat to mountain areas where it is difficult for their enemies to follow them.

▼ Afghan fighters, known as *Mujahideen*, pose for a photo in the Hindu Kush Mountains. *Mujahideen* leaders have been fighting each other ever since the Soviet army left Aghanistan in 1989.

Settlements and Houses

Mountain villages are not found on the very steepest slopes or at the summit. They often grow up in the valley bottom, where the climate is more sheltered and where there is flat, fertile land to build on and to farm. Settlements were usually built on south-facing slopes so that they will catch the sun, even in winter. More settlements are found on the windward side of a mountain range, where there is plenty of water, than in the dry rain-shadow area (see page 8).

Larger villages and towns have sprung up at the wide mouths of valleys, where there is easy access to the lowlands or to other valleys. In the Alps, Innsbruck in Austria and Grenoble in France are examples of larger mountain towns that grew up where two valleys joined.

In the Shadow of the Volcano

People have built settlements on the sides of volcanoes all over the world. Volcanic soil is particularly fertile, so the land is prized by farmers. However, if a volcano erupts, the settlements may be threatened by flows of lava or clouds of volcanic gas and dust.

At 12,000 ft. (3,630 m), La Paz, ▶ the capital of Bolivia, is the highest capital city in the world.

Villages at risk

Special dangers threaten settlements in the mountains. Villages built below steep mountain slopes are in danger from landslides and from avalanches. Avalanches occur particularly in spring and winter. In the Alps and many other mountain areas, people have built fences or planted bands of trees on steep slopes to protect the villages from avalanches. In spring, when the snow begins to melt on mountain tops, swollen streams and rivers can sweep houses away.

▲ During an avalanche, thousands of tons of snow and ice break away from the mountainside and cascade onto the land below.

Summer dwellings

In the Pyrenees and other mountain areas, settlers have built simple huts on the mountain slopes high above the village. In summer, these huts are home for herders tending sheep in the high pastures. Other buildings, often made of stone, are used for storing hay and grain. In winter, these buildings are deserted and may lie under several feet of snow. Nowadays, some are rented out to tourists. Where this has happened, especially in Europe and the United States, house prices sometimes rise so much that it becomes difficult for local people to buy houses.

Building styles

In European mountains, houses are often built with steep, sloping roofs, which prevent snow building up and becoming too heavy. In places where there is a shortage of land, such as the Hunza Valley in the Karakoram Mountains, Pakistan, the roofs of houses are often flat. In the summer, the roofs are used as living space and for drying and storing fruit, vegetables, and firewood.

▼ These simple chalets in the high Swiss Alps are used by herders in the summer. The one on the right is used to store firewood and as shelter for the dairy cattle.

Building materials

Because of the cost and difficulty of bringing materials up to mountain areas, homes are usually built from local materials such as stone and wood from the forests. In the Alps, chalets and farmhouses are traditionally built of local timber and roofed with tiles or slate.

In Nepal, houses are built of mud and stone, with mud floors and thatched or slate roofs. Carved wooden ladders propped against outside walls lead to roofs and upper floors.

Inside a Sherpa House
A visitor to the Himalayas in the 1960s advised: "Never wander into a Sherpa house after dark without a light. If you are not eaten at the door by a ferocious Tibetan dog, you are apt to fall over a sheep or be butted by a yak."

Mobile homes

Some mountain people are nomads, regularly moving their sheep and goats to new grazing land. In Tibet and Mongolia, nomads visit certain grazing sites with their herds at the same time every year. Their homes are round tents, called yurts; they are made of felt and canvas stretched over a framework of poles.

▲ In the Altai Mountains of central Asia, yurts have to be sturdy enough to withstand 100 mph (160 kph) winds. Yurts can be taken down and put up quickly and easily and carried by pack animals to the next site.

Work in the Mountains

Most mountain peoples work as farmers, but mountain farmers do not have easy lives. The short summers and long, cold winters limit the kinds of crops that can be grown, and the soil is often thin and stony. Animals provide milk for drinking and for making butter and cheese. Cheese is particularly valued because it keeps well and is easy to transport.

In the Alps and the Rocky Mountains, farmers keep dairy cattle on the rich meadows of the lower mountain slopes. The grass there is also cut and stored as hay, to feed the animals in winter. The sparse grass of the higher pastures is suitable only for sheep and goats. In the Andes, herds of llamas and alpacas roam the mountains. Their wool can be spun and used to make warm clothing.

▲ In the winter, many Alpine farmers keep their cattle down in the valley in a barn near the farm.

▼ Shepherds in the Hindu Kush Mountains in Afghanistan. Someone must stay with the herds all summer to make sure they are safe and do not stray.

Farming the Mountainsides

On mountainsides in Asia and South America, farmers shore up the soil with stone walls to make flat terraces. This makes the land easier to work and to water. Farmers usually work the land with simple tools such as hand hoes and plows pulled by oxen. In wealthy mountain regions, farmers spread fertilizers on the soil to make it richer and spray their crops to control insect pests.

▲ Plowing a steep slope in the Himalayas using a team of yaks

In mountain regions where the soil is poor, farmers can grow enough food to feed their families but have no surplus to sell for profit. In countries such as Nepal, there is so little money to be made by farming that many men leave their homes to join the army or to seek work in the lowlands.

▲ In the high Andes of Bolivia, surplus vegetables and cloth are traded at local markets.

Forestry

Tree-cutting provides work for people in some mountain areas. Felling trees is hard and sometimes dangerous work. In the highlands of Papua New Guinea in Southeast Asia, tropical hardwood trees such as teak and mahogany are cut down, often by international companies, who make large profits from the sale of these precious timbers.

Coca in the Andes

Many people in the Andes grow a plant called coca. Traditionally it is chewed to ward off hunger and exhaustion. It is also used to make an illegal drug called cocaine. Coca is easy to grow and big profits can be made, although they rarely help the local people. The governments in Bolivia, Peru, and Colombia offer people money to stop growing coca and plant other crops instead.

Gold in the Hills

In 1896, gold was discovered in the mountains of the Klondike, in northwest Canada. Thousands of hopeful prospectors traveled to this remote region and crossed the mountains to claim some of the gold. But few found gold, and many died in the bitter cold.

Mining

Mining provides work for mountain people in many areas. Rocks such as slate and granite make useful building materials. In regions such as the Alps, they have been quarried for hundreds of years. Austria was also a center for mining copper, iron, and silver in ancient and medieval times. In Bolivia, South America, silver mines in the Cerro Rico ("rich mountain") area were once run by the Spanish *conquistadors*. They are still worked today for low-grade silver ore.

▲ A man panning for gold in the Yukon River, Canada, in the Klondike Gold Rush of 1899

▼ Silver miners at Cerro Rico, in the Bolivian Andes. Their work is very tiring because the air is very thin this high up in the mountains (see page 9).

Industry

In Europe and North America, local industries have grown up in mountain regions. In the past, transportation difficulties made it hard for people of mountain areas to sell goods as cheaply as those from lowland regions. So in the Alps and elsewhere, they chose to make special goods that were not produced in other areas and that could be sold at high prices.

Until the early 1900s, the Swiss Alps were an important center for cloth-weaving and embroidery. Switzerland is also famous for making clocks and watches and for its cheeses and fine chocolates. Today, these goods are still produced in the Alps, but in modern factories and with the help of new technology and efficient transportation. Factories in Austria produce glassware and high-quality lenses and other optical equipment. Liechtenstein, a tiny Alpine country, is the world's leading producer of false teeth.

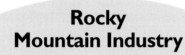

▲ Large cheeses are made from the milk of cows that graze on rich Alpine pastures.

Rocky Mountain Industry

The city of Denver, Colorado, grew up in the 1860s as a center for traders and prospectors. Later, it was a stopping place for stagecoaches and railroads. The city is now a thriving business center with a new international airport. It is also the home of the largest mint in the United States, which produces 75 percent of all American coins.

▼ Denver is nicknamed the "mile-high city," because it is over a mile (1.6 km) above sea level, at the foot of the Rocky Mountains.

Modern transportation systems have opened up the world's high places to tourists as well as to local people. Tourism (see pages 36–41) now provides jobs for a great many people in mountain areas throughout the world.

Hydroelectricity

Rushing torrents and powerful rivers are plentiful in the mountains. They can be used to provide power in the form of hydroelectricity. In more economically developed countries, many streams and rivers have been dammed, and hydroelectric power plants have been built. For local mountain people, hydroelectricity has some disadvantages. The lakes created by the dams may occupy fertile land on the valley floor once used for farming. Sometimes whole villages must be moved to make way for lakes and reservoirs.

Hydroelectric projects, ▶ like this one in Norway, help lowland areas near mountains by bringing cheap electricity and drinking water to their cities.

Transportation and Communication

High mountain ranges form barriers to travel and communication, which have often meant that mountain areas are the last to be developed. In the past, journeys could only be made in summer, when the high passes were free of snow. Some poorer countries still have few roads today.

▲ In remote parts of Europe, donkeys are still used to carry freight through rough mountain country.

Transportation without roads

In the Himalayas, rough roads end in the foothills of the mountains. Donkeys carry some goods along mountain paths, but everything else, including building materials and bulky furniture—even old or injured people—is carried by human porters. In these regions, guest houses have sprung up in villages a day's walk apart, to provide the porters with food and lodgings for the night. In Nepal, these are called *bhattis*, after the word meaning "rice," which is the staple diet. A porter can measure his journey in the number of rice stops he needs to make to complete the trip.

Crossing the water

Fast-flowing streams and rivers also present difficulties for mountain travelers. In poorer countries, simple hoists may be used to winch goods, people, and animals slowly over rushing streams. Trees are sometimes cut to build flimsy bridges, or rope bridges may be slung across the torrent. These fragile structures are often swept away in floods or landslides and must frequently be rebuilt.

A man crossing a simple rope ▶ bridge in the Kashmir Himalayas, northern India

▼ Porters in Nepal carry loads of up to 110 lb. (50 kg) each in baskets on their backs.

Box Winches
In the Karakoram Mountains, part of the Himalayas, simple "box-winches," known as **ghraris,** are used to carry passengers 330 ft. (100 m) across the deep Indus gorge. A shallow wooden box is suspended on two wire ropes, 200 ft. (60 m) above the river. The box is pulled along using a steel cable and pulley.

Traveling by road

In most parts of the world today, modern roads and railroads make travel in the mountains easy compared with the past. Smooth highways zigzag up to passes in the Alps, the Pyrenees, and the Rocky Mountains. Tight, hairpin bends make the roads less steep.

Tunnels

Tunnels mean that some mountain roads can stay open all year round. The Mont Blanc tunnel is 8 mi. (11.5 km) long and joins Chamonix in France to the Aosta Valley in Italy. Miners worked on its construction for four years, during which time seventeen men died. When the tunnel was opened in the 1960s, more than 450,000 vehicles and 100,000 tons of cargo passed through it during the first year.

In winter, snowplows and snowmobiles struggle to keep the high routes open. At the Col de l'Iseran, the highest pass in the Alps, cars pass between walls of snow 30 ft. (9 m) high on either side of the route. Drivers put chains on their vehicles' wheels to prevent them from skidding on icy patches. Snow still blocks some routes altogether, causing villages to be cut off for weeks or even months.

Today, the Alps are crossed by several highways, including the six-lane route between Austria and Italy, which crosses the mountains at the Brenner Pass. Here, a great bridge called the Europa Bridge carries motorway traffic across the pass. These major routes help with problems of traffic buildup, but they can also cause pollution.

◀ Hairpin bends on a French mountain road

▼ Passengers, luggage, and even animals often ride on the roofs of buses traveling on the Karakoram Highway, which crosses the Karakoram Mountains between Pakistan and China.

BLN 2795

29

Railroads

Railroads have made mountain areas more accessible. The highest railroad in Europe runs between Interlaken in Switzerland and a peak called the Jungfrau. The terminus at Jungfraujoch, at 11,332 ft. (3,454 m), is near the summit of the mountain.

▲ This train is on the highest railroad in Europe, in the Swiss Alps. During the steep climb up the Jungfrau, it stops in view of the north face of the Eiger, a sheer rock wall on which many climbers have died.

Cable cars provide an easy means of reaching villages and mountain stations hundreds of feet above the valley. During the summer, the cable cars are shared with walkers and sightseers. In winter, local people are often crammed in with skiers and snowboarders.

Air travel

Millions of visitors now travel to the world's mountain areas by airplane. Airplanes cannot solve all of the problems of mountain travel, however. Visitors arriving by air at La Paz in Bolivia, the world's highest capital, often suffer from mountain sickness because their bodies do not have time to adjust to the high altitude.

▼ Small planes like this keep mountain areas supplied with food and essential supplies.

Helicopters

Helicopters now drop supplies at mountain refuges and villages in the Alps and Pyrenees that were once supplied by donkey trains. Helicopters may be as cheap to run as donkeys, according to pilots in the Alps, who claim: "You feed the animal all year, but the machine eats only when it works." Helicopters are also used for mountain rescue and by doctors visiting their patients.

▲ A helicopter rushes to rescue stranded walkers in Zermatt, in the Swiss Alps.

Telecommunications

Many mountain regions are linked to other areas by telephone. However, when landslides and avalanches destroy lines in remote places, the damage may take months to repair. When this happens, radio may be the only way for villagers to contact the outside world.

Daily Life and Leisure

Change comes more slowly to mountain areas because of their isolation. In the past, mountain people had less money and poorer health than the people of the lowlands. Today, however, in wealthy countries, these difficulties have been largely overcome. Mountain people now share many leisure facilities and modern conveniences enjoyed by lowland people.

In the foothills of mountains in Europe and the United States, modern life has caught up with major cities such as Zurich and Grenoble in the Alps and Denver in the Rocky Mountains. In these cities and in smaller mountain towns, people work in modern offices and factories and enjoy climbing, walking, and skiing in their spare time.

▼ A mountaineer in the Rocky Mountains. Some people in wealthier countries have moved closer to the mountains so that they can enjoy their favorite sports on weekends.

In many poorer countries, however, conditions are harsh, and mountain people still live simple lives. Most of the day is spent working long hours in the fields or forests, especially in the summer. In the winter, there is less work to do and more free time.

▲ Tibetans light a fire for making tea. Yak butter is added to it, instead of milk, which gives it a salty taste.

Nomads at Rest

Daily life is hard for nomadic peoples such as the Ngari, who live on the high plateau-land of Tibet. Although their religion, Buddhism, has been suppressed in the rest of China, Buddhist belief remains strong among the Tibetans. They are a hardy people who relish their free time, which is spent with the family and in prayer. During the long, dark days of winter, Tibetan families gather around the stove. Family members sing and tell long stories and jokes. The women spin wool to make brightly colored clothes.

Fairs and feasts

In the Himalayas, the Alps, and many other mountain regions, local people hold special celebrations to welcome the return of the herds from the high pastures. Shepherds travel to fairs held in the valleys, hoping to get a good price for their animals, which have been fattened on rich mountain grass. There may be feasting and dancing and sports contests at which young people can demonstrate their strength and skill. In the Altai Mountains of Mongolia, herders race horses and hold archery and wrestling matches.

▼ Horsemen in traditional dress at the annual Naadam Festival in Mongolia

Diwali

Hinduism is one of the main religions of Nepal. One of the most important Hindu festivals is Diwali in November, the five-day festival of lights. At night, the houses are lit by the tiny, flickering flames of hundreds of oil lamps. On each of the first four days of the festival, a different animal is celebrated: the crow, dog, cow, and bull. On their special day, these animals are decorated with garlands of yellow flowers. The last day celebrates the bond between brothers and sisters. It is a day of gifts and feasting.

▲ A folk festival in Switzerland, where local people dress in traditional Swiss costume and put flowered hats on the cows' heads. The festival is good for the area's tourist industry.

Alpine customs

In the Alps and the Pyrenees, local people have festivals to celebrate the passing seasons. Cattle returning to the valleys for winter are decorated with ribbons and flowers. However, many mountain customs are dying out today. Traditional costumes of the mountains are mainly worn to please the tourists. Only elderly people in a few regions still wear them every day.

Tourism

▲ Tourists in a horse-drawn sleigh in St. Moritz, Switzerland. The town's spring waters are thought to have healing powers and have attracted tourists for nearly 200 years.

Many mountain areas have changed more in the last fifty years than for many centuries. This is mainly because of tourism. The first tourists visited the mountains of Europe hundreds of years ago. They went to springs and wells in mountain valleys where the water was thought to help cure illness. Towns called spas grew up around the springs, with hotels where visitors could stay. Merano in Italy and St. Moritz (above) are examples of spa towns.

Visiting the peaks

Mountaineers were the first people to venture into the unknown and frightening territory of the high mountains. In 1786, a French doctor, Michel-Gabriel Paccard, climbed to the summit of Mont Blanc with a local guide, Jacques Balmat, and took readings to measure its height.

The English artist Edward Whymper was the ▶ first person to climb the Matterhorn, in Switzerland, in 1865. This engraving, which shows his climb, attracted hundreds of tourists to the Alps in the late nineteenth century.

Guides and Porters

Today, expeditions come from all over the world to tackle the high peaks of the Himalayas. These expeditions provide work for local mountain peoples, such as Sherpas in Nepal and Baltis in northern India. They work as porters, carrying supplies and equipment to the base of the mountains and to camps set up on the route to the summit.

The world's highest peaks in the Himalayas were first visited when Nepal was opened to foreigners in 1947. Mount Everest was climbed in 1953. In the Karakoram, the world's second highest mountain, which is called simply K2, was climbed the following year. Today, scaling sheer mountain faces provides new challenges for mountaineers. Hiking along many of the routes first explored by mountaineers is now popular.

◀ A Balti porter carries a heavy load. A recent U.S. expedition to K2, in the Himalayas, employed 350 Balti porters to carry supplies for fourteen climbers.

Summer tourism

Today, millions of tourists flock to the world's high places every year. In summer, many go to enjoy their favorite sports, whether it is fishing, mountain biking, or hang-gliding. Other, less energetic, visitors can see the sights by car or bus. In wealthier countries, cable cars, mountain railroads, and boats and hydrofoils on lakes allow everyone to enjoy the scenery.

Cool
Mountain Air

In summer in some parts of the world, the coolness of the mountains offers a welcome relief from the heat of the lowlands. Simla is a hill resort in northern India that became popular during the eighteenth and nineteenth centuries when India was part of the British Empire. The cool mountain air attracted British officials and their families, who were unused to the intense heat of the Indian summers. It remains a popular tourist spot today.

All these visitors need places to stay. In the last fifty years, many mountain villages have grown into large resorts with hotels and restaurants, which provide employment for local people. Walking and nature vacations are popular in many mountain regions today. Trekkers carrying backpacks walk in the mountains of New Zealand, or hike the Inca Trail in the Andes, which leads to Machu Picchu.

▼ Mountain bikers near Chamonix, in the French Alps

In the Alps and other European mountains, walkers stay in mountain huts, called refuges, that provide a bed and an evening meal after a hard day's hiking. Some refuges can take as many as a hundred visitors. In Nepal, many porters' guest houses have now become tourist hotels.

▲ A trekkers' camp in Nepal

Problems with tourism

Large numbers of tourists bring litter and pollution to the mountains. In Nepal, litter has recently become a problem on the most popular walking routes to Mount Everest and around Mount Annapurna in the west. Tourists visit these remote mountain areas to see unspoiled natural scenery. Yet their coming sometimes destroys the beauty for everyone.

▼ Yosemite National Park has about 2.5 million visitors a year. In order to protect the fragile mountain areas within the park, the number of visitors allowed in particular areas is strictly controlled.

Winter sports

Mountains are also popular destinations for winter holidays. Winter sports include tobogganing, ice skating, and, most recently, snowboarding. Since the 1960s, skiing has done more to open up and change mountain areas than any other form of tourism. Cross-country skiing was first developed by the peoples of Scandinavia. Downhill skiing began in the 1930s and is now extremely popular.

Local people welcome the skiers for many reasons. Ski tourism provides jobs for many mountain people, who find work as shop assistants, hotel staff, waiters, guides, and ski instructors. The work is particularly welcome in winter, when there is less work on farms and in villages. Skiers are high-spending tourists, who rent expensive equipment and enjoy the local nightlife after the day's skiing.

▲ Ski resorts bring many changes to mountain areas. Chair lifts and cable cars are needed to ferry skiers up the mountains. In the valleys, hotels, chalets, shops, and bars are built.

Tourist Numbers

Over 12 million tourists visit the Alps every year. Most are happy to see the sights by car or bus. In contrast, only a few thousand tourists hike in the Himalayas in Nepal during the same period. Most visit during spring and autumn, when the high peaks can be clearly seen. There are few facilities for tourists in Nepal.

Preparing the slopes

Ski trails are specially prepared ski routes down mountainsides. Trees are cut down, usually on the lower slopes, to make clear, safe paths to ski down. Trees protect the soil on steep mountain slopes because their roots anchor the earth and prevent it from washing away in heavy rain. Stripped of this natural protection, mountain slopes erode more quickly. Because of this, landslides and avalanches occur more often on slopes that have been prepared for skiing.

▲ Snowboarding is becoming a popular winter sport.

▼ Many people enjoy skiing, but ski trails harm the mountain slopes. The earth is damaged by the machines that prepare the trails and by the tracks of skis.

The Future

The future of mountain people around the world depends on the future of the mountains themselves. These mighty masses of rock may seem eternal and unchanging, but they are fragile places for people, plants, and animals to live. They are easily harmed and must be managed carefully.

Leaving the mountains

In parts of the Alps and the Pyrenees, people are leaving the mountains. Tourism cannot create enough jobs for everyone, so many young people go to the lowlands in search of jobs and lifestyles suited to towns or cities. Some villages have been abandoned altogether. In many others, old people remain, but there are too few families. The answer to this problem may lie in providing more jobs and better facilities, such as social centers for villagers and not just attractions for the tourists.

▼ A deserted village near Aragon, in the Spanish Pyrenees

Too many people

Some mountain regions in poorer countries experience problems caused by rapidly growing populations. This puts a much greater pressure on the countryside than a population increase in the lowlands, where there is plenty of land to farm. Mountain people cut down the trees for fuel or strip their leaves to feed the animals. In some areas the wood is sold for profit or used as fuel to heat water.

▲ A Nepalese family collecting firewood to use as fuel

National parks

In many parts of the world, national parks have been set up to help preserve the mountains. The plants and animals that live there are protected and are disturbed as little as possible. The oldest park in the United States was set up 100 years ago, at Yellowstone in the Rocky Mountains, a region of natural hot springs. Tourists visiting national parks are encouraged to learn about and respect the wildlife. They are asked to "Take nothing but photos, leave nothing but footprints."

Some national parks in the United States, Canada, and elsewhere are large enough to form true areas of wilderness, where mountain animals can roam freely. Other parks, particularly in Europe, are relatively small, but still receive thousands of visitors each year. Large numbers of tourists put great pressure on these natural areas.

▲ A lynx in the vast Chang Tang wildlife preserve, on the high plateau of Tibet. The preserve was set up in 1996.

Poisoned Trees

Modern roads and highways cause problems in the mountains. Pollution from factories and exhaust from cars and trucks have damaged forests in Switzerland and other European countries, and many trees are dying. The Swiss Government plans to build two new rail routes through the mountains, to help reduce the problems of pollution and traffic buildup.

◀ Summer walkers in the Swiss Alps. Grass, thin soil, and rocks in popular tourist spots are quickly worn away by the feet of walkers. In some national parks paved paths have been built to protect the fragile soil and rock.

Planning for the future

In both rich and poorer countries, mountain areas need to be protected and properly looked after. Governments could spend more on mountain villages, to provide better health care and more jobs and schools. In European mountains, tourist developments have to be carefully managed. Overdevelopment can spoil the scenery and transform villages from real communities into pretty places for visitors to photograph.

In poorer countries, local people may need money from richer countries to help them preserve their mountain regions. Nowadays, most foreign projects help local people in ways that fit in with their own traditions. If mountain areas are well managed, they will be safe for the enjoyment of future tourists and for the wildlife and people who live there.

▼ This is a tiny hydroelectric power plant in Nepal. A small waterwheel generates electricity through the hut and out along the wires.

Glossary

Alpacas South American pack animals, prized for their silky fleece.

Altitude Height above sea level.

Archaeologist Someone who studies ancient sites.

Avalanches Falling masses of snow and rock.

Cable cars Cabins, suspended from cables, that carry passengers up and down mountains.

Conquistadors The Spanish conquerors of Mexico and Peru in the sixteenth century.

Dialect The local version of a language.

Eroded Worn away by natural forces such as frost, wind, snow, and ice. Erosion takes place more quickly once plants that protect the soil have been removed.

Fertilizers Chemicals put on the soil to make it more fertile.

Glacier A slow-moving mass of ice on a mountain.

Humid Warm and damp weather conditions.

Hydroelectricity Electricity generated through the power of running water.

Landslides Falling masses of rock and soil.

Llamas South American pack animals, which are members of the camel family.

Medieval The period of history from about A.D. 900 to A.D. 1500.

Mint A building where banknotes and coins are made.

Mummified A dead body that has been preserved.

Neanderthals Prehistoric people.

Nomads People who travel with their herds in search of fresh pastureland.

Pass A lower point between high mountains, used by travelers.

Pesticides Strong chemicals used on crops to kill insects.

Pioneers People who are the first to explore and settle a new land or territory.

Prevailing wind The wind that most commonly blows in an area.

Prospectors People who explore a region in search of valuable minerals such as gold.

Quarried Removed from the ground.

Rain shadow The area of a mountain facing away from the main, prevailing winds. It receives very little rain.

Ranges Groups of mountains.

Reservoirs Artificial lakes formed by damming a river.

Summits Mountain tops, or peaks.

Terraces Steps cut into the hillside to make more space for farming.

Vicuñas A wild type of llama. They have very fine wool.

Yaks Hairy cattle found in the mountains of Asia.

Further Information

Books to read

Barnes-Svarney, Patricia L. *Born of Heat and Pressure: Mountains and Metamorphic Rocks* (Earth Processes). Springfield, NJ: Enslow Publishers, 1991.

Bradley, Catherine. *Life in the Mountains*. New York: Scholastic, 1993.

Bramwell, Martyn. *Mountains* (Earth Science Library). Danbury, CT: Franklin Watts, 1994.

Cumming, David. *Mountains* (Habitats). Austin, TX: Thomson Learning, 1995.

Facklam, Howard and Margery Facklam. *Avalanche!* (Nature's Disasters). Parsippany, NJ: Silver Burdett Press, 1991.

Simon, Seymour. *Mountains*. New York: Morrow Junior Books, 1994.

Van Rose, Susanna. *Volcano and Earthquake* (Eyewitness). New York: Knopf Books for Young Readers, 1992.

Vogt, Gregory. *Volcanoes*. Brookfield, CT: Millbrook Press, 1994.

Williams, Lawrence. *Mountains* (Last Frontiers). Tarrytown, NY: Marshall Cavendish, 1990.

CD Roms
Exploring Land Habitats (Steck-Vaughn)

Violent Earth (Steck-Vaughn)

Useful addresses

You can find more information about mountains, and the people who live in them, if you write to the following organizations:

Earth Living Foundation
P.O. Box 188
Hesperus, CO 81326
(970) 385-5500

Friends of the Earth
1025 Vermont Avenue NW
Suite 300
Washington, D.C. 20005-6303
(202) 783-7400

Greenpeace U.S.A.
1436 U Street, NW
Washington, D.C. 20009

World Wildlife Fund
1250 24th Street NW
P.O. Box 96555
Washington, D.C. 20077-7795

Picture acknowledgments
The publisher would like to thank the following for allowing their pictures to be used in this book: Abbot Hall, Kendal 13; Axiom *Title page*, chapter headings, 19, 33; Britstock 34; Bruce Coleman *Cover*; David Cumming 42; Environmental Images 43; Eye Ubiquitous 14 (bottom), 20 (top), 29 David Cumming, 37 (bottom); Hulton Getty 14 (top), 23 (top); Image Bank 4, 40; Impact 12, 15, 27 (top), 27 (bottom); James Davis Worldwide 30 (top and bottom), 35, 39 (top); Mary Evans Picture Library 37 (top); Panos 5 (bottom), 16, 20 (top), 21 (top), 22 (top), 23 (bottom), 41, 45 (bottom); Pictor 9, 26, 31; Stockfile 38; Switzerland Tourism 18, 24 (top), 45 (top); Tony Stone 3, 7, 17, 24 (bottom), 25, 32, 39 (bottom), 41 (top), 41 (bottom), 44; Wayland Picture Library 10; Zefa 5 (top), 11.

Index